Good Painting

PAINTING
WITHOUT FAINTING
By Don Aslett

ACKNOWLEDGMENTS

Thanks to all the pros, semi-pros, and frustrated (and inspired) amateurs who gave me ideas and input, including Larry, Rick, and Rell Aslett, Nolan Mecham, Jeff England, Mark Browning, Rulon Parker, and Carol Cartaino.

A big nod of appreciation, too, to all the manufacturers of quality paint.

Painting Without Fainting
Copyright © 1994 by Don A. Aslett. Illustrations copyright © 1994 Don A. Aslett. Printed and bound in the United States of America. All rights reserved. No part of this book may be reproduced in any form or by any electronic or mechanical means including information storage and retrieval systems without permission in writing from the publisher, except by a reviewer, who may quote brief passages in a review.
Published by Marsh Creek Press, PO Box 700, Pocatello, Idaho 83204; 208-232-3535

ISBN 0-937750-09-3

Illustrator, Designer: Craig LaGory
Illustrator: Kerry Otteson
Editor: Carol Cartaino
Production Manager: Tobi Haynes

MARSH CREEK PRESS

ALSO BY DON ASLETT

Professional Cleaning Books:
Cleaning Up for a Living
The Professional Cleaner's Personal Handbook
How to Upgrade & Motivate Your Cleaning Crews
Construction Cleanup
Don Aslett's Professional Cleaner's Clip Art
Painting Without Fainting

How to Clean:
Is There Life After Housework?
Do I Dust or Vacuum First?
Make Your House Do the Housework
Don Aslett's Clean in a Minute
Who Says It's a Woman's Job to Clean?
Pet Clean-Up Made Easy
Don Aslett's Stainbuster's Bible
The Cleaning Encyclopedia

More help with Personal Management:
How to Have a 48-Hour Day
How to Handle 1,000 Things at Once

Help for Packrats:
Clutter's Last Stand
Not for Packrats Only
Clutter Free! Finally & Forever
The Office Clutter Cure

Business Books:
Keeping Work Simple
How to be #1 With Your Boss
Everything I Needed to Know About Business
    I Learned in the Barnyard
Speak Up!

TABLE OF CONTENTS

Can you paint faster and better?

Some speed stories to make you a believer

At nineteen I hardly knew what a paintbrush was. Any experience I had with painting, up to that point, was synonymous with MESS. Nothing worked the way it was supposed to, it was a fight, awful. In the opinions and observations of 99% of others, too, painting was a loser job all the way, whether painting a piece of machinery, a high school banner, or a barn. It basically meant smearing an opaque liquid on an unruly surface (including yourself), and ending up smelling like a can of thinner for at least a week after the job was done.

While attending college I organized my own company, and in two years built it into a nice little business—cleaning, waxing, and washing ahead of painters. And then it happened. I hired Nolan Mecham, a student getting his MBA. He was a real painter. When one of our customers, deeply impressed by our brilliant cleaning job, asked if we would paint her living room, Nolan said "Yes" (though I couldn't help thinking it looked like a week's job). I served as Nolan's flunky, and in three hours it was done—beautiful, even, not a drip anywhere. It was like magic when you controlled the paint. Thus my second great love was born, and my company began painting regularly, all over town and all over the state. Applying what I learned from Nolan and other pros, paint stores, and experience, it was a thrill to renew old surfaces and make things look fresh and sharp and new.

We became licensed paint contractors, and I've painted professionally now for more than thirty-five years. I'd rather paint than golf or sit in a in hot tub, go to the beach or out to dinner. And I've brought a number of paint-haters around to my way of thinking.

PAINTING IS DYNAMIC AND FUN

...And profitable. Knowing how to paint has saved me over $100,000 in my personal life alone, and as a business it's earned me millions. My two sons, too, have now added professional painting to their other professional skills.

 My son Grant, to the amazement of a college "facility maintenance" class I was teaching, painted an entire room right before their eyes in 25 minutes... including cleanup!

 I saw 28-year-old Mark Browning and two other painters do a beautiful $50,000 painting job on ten huge Sun Valley condos in 22 days.

1

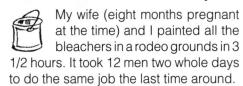

What's the secret?

These people knew the professional way to paint, which I PROMISE you will learn in just a few minutes of reading!

 My wife (eight months pregnant at the time) and I painted all the bleachers in a rodeo grounds in 3 1/2 hours. It took 12 men two whole days to do the same job the last time around.

 I painted four large county fair buildings in a single afternoon, with an airless sprayer and fifty gallons of white paint.

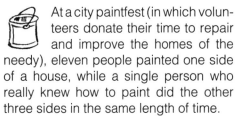 Two junior high schoolers who had never painted before became excellent, sought-after painters after just one summer of working with and learning from our crew.

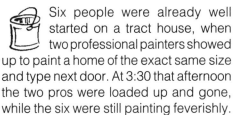 At a city paintfest (in which volunteers donate their time to repair and improve the homes of the needy), eleven people painted one side of a house, while a single person who really knew how to paint did the other three sides in the same length of time.

Six people were already well started on a tract house, when two professional painters showed up to paint a home of the exact same size and type next door. At 3:30 that afternoon the two pros were loaded up and gone, while the six were still painting feverishly.

One time a chain store was painted by a crew of people for $2500. The next year the new tenant hired a 26-year-old pro who showed up on the job alone. "Where's your crew?" the owner asked. "Come back tomorrow night," said the young man, "and you'll see." He did, and the job was not only completed, but beautiful. No crew was needed, because this fellow knew how to paint.

WHY PAINT... AT ALL?

That's easy to answer.

1. Paint slows deterioration and depreciation. Painting saves surfaces—and thus money. With paint you're buying and getting protection. It protects the surface from wear and tear and keeps moisture and the other elements off of wood, metal, and masonry, preventing rust, staining, and rotting.

2. Painting extends the life of things, which is easier on our environment as well as on ourselves. When things are taken care of we don't have to spend energy and resources to replace them.

3. Well painted things can be cleaned much more easily and cheaply. A coat of paint can speed cleaning by up to 50%. Fingerprints, marks, spills, dirt—all will clean quickly off a good painted surface. This will save you a lot of time over a lifetime.

4. Because it enhances appearance, painting increases the value of things. Painting ups the value of your property and tells everyone that YOU CARE. Paint is one of the least expensive and easiest ways to upgrade and improve your home, or anything else.

5. Bright, clean, fresh paint gives us a lift, cheers us up, make us feel better about those interior spaces we spend so much time in. One pro says his most common call to paint is to keep mother-in-laws happy.

6. Painting increases our sense of self-esteem and self-worth. If something is well painted and attractive, we are proud of it and we treat it better. This is true of just about anything we own, drive, live in, or use. And because we look and act better and make a better impression, WE are treated better! All this for a little paint.

7. Painting is an excellent way to earn money, too. There are always paint jobs

around, which we can profit from in cash or personal appreciation.

Knowing how to paint well will do more for your life and outlook than most of the thrill-seeking trivia we engage in.

If it won't clean up, looks bad, needs protection, or you just don't feel good about it… …*PAINT IT!* That means when:

- The surface or object in question is faded, dull, or dirty
- Damaged
- You're depressed or just plain bored by it.

WHEN TO PAINT

(The ideal, so your paint won't peel!)

The Bible tells us there is a time and season for all things—a time to be born and a time to die, a time to reap and a time to sow… and for sure, we can add to that, a time to paint and a time to desist from painting.

Bad timing can and does add lots of misery to any painting job, so don't push it.

The best time to paint is:

1. When the **temperature** is above 60 and below 90 degrees F. Any colder or hotter will adversely affect drying time. The paint will dry too fast or too slow. Unfavorable temperatures can also pre-

vent the paint from bonding properly to the surface. Plus you will be too awkward (too cold and stiff or too overheated) to work smoothly and effectively.

2. When it isn't windy or raining. **Wind and rain** will ruin even perfect work or the most expensive paint.

3. Any time but **winter.** In most areas winter is a time of restricted access and reduced ability to ventilate properly during a job. Winter complicates not only drying but preparation and setup, etc.

In winter, paint with the sun (especially you folks up north).

In summer, paint with the shade.

4. **Early** in the day. This leaves you some overtime in case the job takes longer

than you imagined or you want to go on and do more. There are fewer human and atmospheric disturbances early in the day, too. You are fresh, you have more patience and energy, and the stores are still open in case you find yourself out of something. Starting (and finishing) late really limits you!

5. When there is **low or minimal traffic**, in and around the room, house, structure, or object you need to paint. This means kids, visitors, birds, bugs, pets, construction projects, meals, passersby, etc.

> *Remember a WET PAINT sign is about the most ignored and disrespected thing going, by people, animals, and Mother Nature.*

ELP!?@!..**

(Do you need it?
What kind do you want?)

When it's time to paint (your nerves or the situation can't wait any longer) you basically have three choices:

1. Do it yourself.

2. Get someone to help you.

3. Hire a professional painter.

Choice 1 is all in your hands. Choices 2 and 3 can be a real blessing or your downfall, depending on who, when, and how.

Don't be afraid to call a professional, or at least get an estimate from one, if painting really bothers you. Or if you make $300 a day and would only lose $80 by staying home and doing it yourself in a day of misery.

Whatever you do, bear in mind that NOTHING is worse than:

A relative, friend, student, nephew, grandson, neighbor, or down and out soul who is sincere but can't paint. They will waste time and money,

damage your property, and set you back weeks or worse.

OR a paint contractor who overcharges and undercoats you.

Both of these situations are incredibly common. Painting done badly can almost be as damaging as a fire, flood, or vandalism. You can't just erase or gloss over irresponsible painting.

Any worthwhile help, amateur or pro, will be able to fill out perfectly (not have to guess or estimate) the sheet that follows. Qualified craftsmen know how, and they know how much—money, time, and paint something will take:

ALWAYS:

- Get a firm price/bid
- Get **AND CHECK** references
- Get a firm start and **finish** date
- Find out WHO will do the actual work on the job
- NEVER pay in advance.

If your prospective painter can't provide all of the above, I'd avoid them!

Here's a sample of what should be included in a bid for any painting project.

Contractor or Painter's

Name _____

Address _____

Phone _____

License # _____

This job is ☐ INTERIOR ☐ EXTERIOR painting, as follows.

Job includes:

1. What rooms or areas and what surfaces?

2. Number of coats on each surface

3. Type of paint, paint number and color, for each part of the job.
And what will the source of the paint be (is it a professional source?)

4. Preparation (outline exactly what will be done besides painting—
cleaning, sanding, caulking, repairing, etc.)

5. Equipment and materials ☐ Owner furnishes ☐ Painter furnishes

6. Make sure the contractor has liability insurance (and bonding if
necessary)

7. Total cost and payment schedule (NEVER pay in advance!)

8. Dates (start and finish)

Signatures: Owner_____ Painter_____

WHAT TYPE OF PAINT?

Your choice of paint for a particular area should be based on that area or object's need for:

1. Cleanablity
2. Hiding power
3. Durability
4. Uniformity
(smoothness and ease of application)
5. Elasticity
(will the paint flex and fill a little?)

Paints and primers come in water base (latex) or oil base (alkyd). Nowadays both are fine and good. Your choice comes down to a matter of ease of use, speed of drying time and cleanup, plus good old personal preference, of course.

Don't get psyched out here. Whenever you're in doubt, go to a pro paint store and ASK.

Some paint on some surfaces and in some climates is more attractive and durable. For example, latex breathes better in moisture-ridden conditions. What do the pros use in the situation you're up against? Your local professional paint store personnel will know.

Buy well-known, high-quality brands. Good paint goes farther, covers better, drips less, and lasts longer than the bargain cheapies. The extra $5 spent on a gallon of paint is one of the best cleaning and home improvement investments you'll ever make.

Now a little paint primer:

Primer This will be covered up in the end. Its purpose is to seal the surface and provide a firm base for the finish coat to adhere to. (See p. 21.)

Flat This means the finished surface will absorb light, not reflect it. Flat painted walls look soft and refined, but they mark more easily and are harder to clean. Best for ceilings.

Satin my favorite. Has a low sheen, expensive look. It holds out grease and holds its own against abuse, and is a cinch to clean. "Semigloss" finishes are especially scrubbable. They'll lose their "new" shine in a short time, so don't panic!

"Eggshell" finishes are somewhat flatter and more matte than semigloss.

Gloss The shiny surface reflects a lot of light, which helps keep things looking clean. It does actually make them easy to clean, too.

Gloss painted surfaces are tough and wear well, which makes them great for doors and woodwork. Too much of this kind of paint in one place can create a cheap shiny look, however, and gloss surfaces show blemishes all too well.

7

Latex enamels are great, just make sure you prime the surface first if you're painting over old oil paint, or that new paint will chip off on you!

Epoxy is a whole different category of coating, created (like epoxy glue) from two different components not mixed together until application time.

It has the superior hardness, durability, and adherence otherwise found only in baked-on enamels. Ideal for use in high humidity areas such as bathrooms, but it can't be used just anywhere. It will last, but it's tough stuff to use. Talk to your paint store about it, and if you don't have a real need for it, I'd avoid it.

Clear Coatings There is also a whole spectrum of clear coatings such as varnish and polyurethane. Most of these are prepared for and applied (cleaned up after, too!) the same as oil paint. Here, too, a short visit with paint store personnel can steer you in the right direction.

Do business with professional paint stores. You'll recover any additional cost in the quality of the end result and time (and headaches and heartaches) saved.

| Flat | Eggshell | Satin | Semigloss | High gloss |

WHAT ABOUT MY OLD PAINT?

Fresh old paint, or maybe even old or old-old paint. Well, if you can chisel the lid off (which is doubtful), you'll generally find at least a half-inch scab on top. Then after you ruin a tool or your clothes fishing that out, there's never enough to finish the job. So you mix it with some other old quarter-can remnant, and if the whole thing isn't curdled, you come up with that ever-popular color, vomit beige. (And if you run out of that, Rembrandt himself wouldn't be able to match it!)

FREEZING wrecks latex and acrylic paints. And age and failure to properly seal the container will ruin even oil paint in time. However, if that old paint is of good quality and there's a lot of it and it isn't a senior citizen of storage, **use it.**

Just be sure to:

☐ Check carefully to see if it's water or oil base (if it's been stored in something other than the original container, or there are so many paint drips it's impossible to read the label). If you pour latex into oil, you'll ruin both gallons. Thin it a little. (See p. 22.) Most stored paint has gotten heavy from evaporation.

☐ Stir and stir and stir and stir and stir, then shake, and then for good measure I'd say a little blessing over it. Whatever you do, make sure it's 100% blended before you start to apply it.

☐ Now STRAIN it! We pros use a nylon sock or old pantyhose leg. Then wrap your "strainer" in old newspaper and dispose of it.

☐ If it's the wrong shade, you need it to be lighter or darker, you can add a little lighter or darker paint of the same type, or a little white or black paint of the same type.

☐ Make sure you have enough for the whole project before you start. Remember, there's no color code on this concoction!

Do your best to read the label and see what kind of paint it is. That garage sale or "odd lot" bargain might be wonderful stuff, but specifically designed for something other than what you have in mind. A friend of mine got a great deal on 100 gallons (he had to paint some bleachers). It turned out to be aircraft carrier deck paint containing sand and grit for traction. It ruined not only a $1500 paint gun, but about 10,000 rear ends! Another friend painted his house in a single day with some beautiful leftover white he found in an Army-Navy store at a real bargain. That night he found out why. It was a fluorescent reflective paint, and his house lit up like the U.S. Capitol building when a glimmer of light hit it.

NOW THAT BIG QUESTION

COLOR

Choosing a color for a whole room from a little paint chip has caused many a nervous collapse after the paint is on. Paint is always darker and brighter than what you expected looking at the chip.

I've heard of paint professionals who will paint over a client's painfully chosen paint "chip" with a color they know is better. Then when the customer sees the finished job and is overjoyed with his or her color choice, the painter holds the chip up to the surface and it's a perfect match! (If they saw the color they actually picked, they'd be in agony.)

The best way, by far, to choose a color is not from chips and charts, but by finding somewhere—a house or room—where you can see it in the altogether, already applied. A home or place you like the looks of is one of the best decision makers and about the best way to insure that you'll end up happy.

CHOOSE LIGHTER COLORS

When you get the shade and color you think you want, move a couple of shades lighter on the color chart. You'll probably be much happier with the results. Besides, lighter colors are more cheerful, reduce lighting costs, and simply look and feel cleaner.

Choose lighter colors. Let your drapes, furniture, and carpets accent your home.

Select a reasonable color, and use as much of that same color throughout your home as possible. Too many homes look like an Easter basket because homemakers are still trying to decorate their homes with paint. The color and style of modern furniture, drapes, and carpet do a fine job of giving a home richness and taste. Using a single shade of off white on all the walls, ceilings, and woodwork will allow your furnishings to flatter your home. It will simplify your painting work and it won't go out of style. (And all your touchup paint is in one can.)

A few great truths about color from several thousand years' worth of professional experience

1. Yellow is a tough color to get even coverage with. And yellow kitchens make meat look green!

2. Dark colors absorb sun and heat (and can get hot enough outside to twist or distort beams!).

3. Reds are the most stimulating, but they also fade the most.

4. Grey is an indecisive color.

5. Green (light green) is the most restful to the eyes.

6. Dark accent colors make walls appear to move in and ceilings down toward you.

7. Lighter colors are the easiest to match when you're doing touchup work.

The bottom line is: use lighter colors and as much of the same color as possible.

ow much...
(Paint will it take?)

Estimating this accurately is a Big, BIG part of painting. Running out of paint in the middle or near the end of a job can double its cost (in cash, time, and emotion).

The Golden Rule (of any color)

Buy enough paint! Leftovers cost you about $10 on the average; running out at least $85. Add to that frustration all-too-visible stop and start lines, the problems of paint matching, what all this does to the schedule, and you can trust me when I say: BUY ENOUGH PAINT!

Three quarts often cost as much as a gallon, and quarts are harder to use. Plus unopened cans of standard colors can usually be returned.

Paint will cover at least 300 and on smooth easy walls sometimes up to 800 square feet per gallon. So if you have a 1500 square foot room to do, do you buy five gallons, or two? That's quite a difference, and could mean a lot of waste.

To find out:

First Read the label on the paint container—different paints cover differently.

Second How good is the paint? Good paints cover at least a third more than cheapos.

Third How porous is the surface? New surfaces are usually much more porous than old ones, and can suck up a lot of paint.

Fourth How many coats are you going to give it?

How to figure out how much paint you need

First, determine the square footage of the room by adding up the length of all the walls and multiplying that number by the height of the room from floor to ceiling.

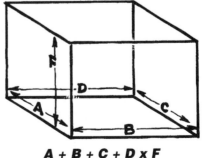

$$A + B + C + D \times F$$

11

If you use a different paint for doors and trim, don't forget to subtract your doors (approximately 21 square feet each for a standard door) and windows (multiply the height of each window by the width) from the total.

The square footage of the ceiling is simply the length of the room times the width.

Divide your wall total by the area one gallon of that particular paint will cover. The result is the number of gallons required for one coat.

If you feel insecure about your arithmetic, take the room measurements to your paint dealer and let him or her tell you how much!

Second or third coats generally take a little less paint than the first coat.

WHAT ABOUT TIME, NOW?

A lot harder to estimate. Preparation (cleaning and covering things, moving them out of the way) usually takes as much—or more—time than the actual painting. How heavily furnished the area is, what condition the surface is in (what kind of patching or repairs it needs), what kind of woodwork or other trim is involved—all make a difference.

THE TOOLS...

Of the paint pros for you!

You'll need them if you really intend to charge into painting like a professional and do it faster (much faster) and easier (much easier) than you've ever done before (as well as cheaper and with hardly a mess at all when you're through). Professional tools cost a little more but

- They last much longer
- And work at least 50% better and faster.

Or as one pro painter put it, after looking at the discount-store tools one client asked him to use: "Lady, I'm the best painter in the state, but using this stuff I'll do a terrible job, and it will take twice the time, and hold up only half as long."

Buy Good Tools
Buy Good Tools
Buy Good TOOLS!

Leave the gadgets and gizmos alone—paper buckets, sponge brushes, pad applicators, throwaway rollers and roller trays and all the rest.

Serious professional paint stores have serious professional tools. Variety and discount stores are full of painting toys and novelties and flimsy one-timers.

THE BIG BASICS WHEN BUYING

First you have to address that big mystery of painthood—should I brush, roll, or spray it on?

Spraying (see p. 41) is never as simple as it seems. Unless you've had a lot of experience with it, I'd avoid it until you've had a chance to work with or around a professional sprayer. Then you'll be ready.

Good pros usually do a brush and roller combination. I brush the edges and corners, but beyond that I roll almost everything, and brush right behind the roller where I don't want stipples or that orange peel roller texture. Handled properly, a roller gets the paint on quickly and evenly—when you're dipping and strok-ing with a brush, it takes a long time to transfer paint out of a bucket onto a wall.

Exactly what do you need now?

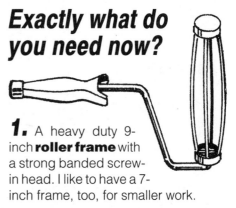

1. A heavy duty 9-inch **roller frame** with a strong banded screw-in head. I like to have a 7-inch frame, too, for smaller work.

2. Roller cover. A thicker one holds more paint and reaches into tiny uneven spots and depressions better. It's also less likely to slip and slide on the surface. Most pros prefer a 3/8–1/2-inch nap for smooth surfaces and 1-inch for rough ones. The real short nap type (sometimes called "candy stripe") are good for varnish.

Roller covers come in different pile or nap lengths. It's important to choose the right pile for the surface you're painting.

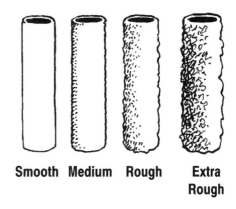

Smooth   Medium   Rough   Extra Rough

Follow these guidelines:

SURFACE	PILE
SMOOTH For walls, floors, fine finishing	3/16", 1/4"
MEDIUM The all-around best covering size; will give a mildly textured finish to a smooth wall	3/8", 1/2"
ROUGH For lightly stuccoed or textured surfaces and masonry floors	3/4"
EXTRA ROUGH For brick, block, masonry, stucco.	1"

There are also special rollers designed for acoustic ceilings.

Be cautious of rolling those "cottage cheese" (soft acoustical fleck) ceilings. You usually have to spray them the first time they're painted, to seal and stabilize them. Then the next time you can use a roller.

3. A **roller screen** and a **5-gallon plastic bucket.** These are inexpensive and far superior to a roller pan for use with any size roller.

The 5-gallon bucket, which you can often get for free, holds more (a couple of

gallons as opposed to a couple of quarts). It's easier to move from place to place, and less likely to be spilled or stumbled over. In a bucket, your paint won't dry on you while you're working with it (and if you have to take a break you can just drape a wet cloth over the top of the bucket). When painting from a ladder, you can refill your roller from the bucket without getting down off the ladder. A bucket even makes cleanup easier and neater, and gives you a handy place to store your paint tools when you're done.

4. **Extension handle.** Any that will screw into your roller will work, but the little Wooster metal and fiberglass model that expands from 2 to 4 feet at the click of a button is hard to beat. It's available at paint stores.

5. Buy a good 2 1/2-inch angled **sash brush** for trim, and for most other interior brush work a 3-inch **straight brush**.

Nylon or polyester bristle brushes work well with either oil base or latex paints. Natural bristle (usually 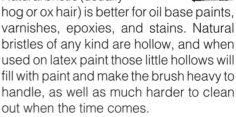 hog or ox hair) is better for oil base paints, varnishes, epoxies, and stains. Natural bristles of any kind are hollow, and when used on latex paint those little hollows will fill with paint and make the brush heavy to handle, as well as much harder to clean out when the time comes.

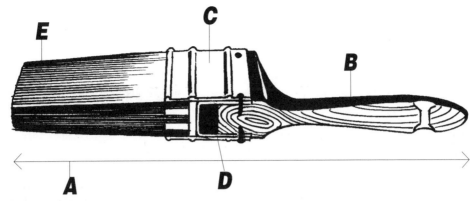

BUYING THE RIGHT BRUSH

Always inspect a brush before you buy it. Remove the cover or packaging and check it closely for the following:

A. Size Match the brush to the job. In general, the bigger and rougher the job, the larger brush you'll want to use. Bigger brushes carry more paint and cover more area. On the other hand, your own size and ability to handle a particular brush is important too. You'll spill less, drip less, and get less tired using a brush you're comfortable with.

B. Handle A well designed handle is smooth and carefully balanced to offset the weight of the bristles when loaded with paint, making all your brushing motions easier. Hold the brush you're considering in your hand—women often prefer the pencil-sized handles, and men the larger, thicker ones, for a better grip.

Pro paintbrushes leave all that glitzy paint and varnish decoration off the handle. It only gets ugly after you've used or cleaned the brush once or twice, anyway.

C. Ferrule (the metal strip wrapped around the bottom of the handle to strengthen it) should be good and solid, and tightly and neatly wound around the brush. It should be attached to the handle securely with screws or other sturdy fasteners.

D. You can't see it, but the tops of the bristles are locked into an **Adhesive** behind the ferrule. You can't pull gobs of bristles out of a good brush.

E. Bristles A good brush has a thick-feeling cluster of bristles that won't easily separate or pull out from the brush.

Bristle LENGTH should vary. To check out a particular brush, run your hand over the bristles. Shorter bristles should pop up first, signaling a mixture of bristle lengths. This will make loading the brush with paint and achieving a smooth finish easier and more reliable.

The best-made bristles also have plenty of split or "flagged" ends, fuzzy tips that instantly spring back into their original position when bent and released. They too, help you achieve a smooth finish.

15

The little extras you DO want:

1. Good **paint rags**—terry or soft cotton cloths are at least ten times better (more absorbent) than most "clothes rags." And don't reuse your paint rags!

A good thick absorbent paper towel like Brawny 100% Recycled, or Scott shop towels, is next best.

2. A stiff sharp **putty chisel**, to skim off excess spackle, scrape up dried paint droplets and bird poop, and open, pry, and cut things. A true painter can even eat lunch with one!

3. A good heavy **dropcloth**, preferably canvas (see p. 23).

4. A 3-inch **trim roller** can make short work of things like sashes, woodwork, and window trim.

5. Paint **stirring sticks**. Always get a couple extra—don't forget you'll be using them to clean your rollers, too.

6. A **metal edger.** Use an edger for painting lap siding where it meets a straight corner board, or for protecting carpet when you paint base molding. Wipe both sides of the edger off with a rag each time you move it so you don't end up smearing paint around.

7. Ah! Now the pro's secret weapon—an

electric fan. Just a little ten or fifteen dollar number will do. They perform an important function by bringing air in or pushing it out of your painting area. This keeps fumes from building up and helps keep you more comfortable. (Do remember that it will inflate your dropcloths if they aren't tucked and tied down tight.)

8. Last, a nice sturdy convenient **container** (with a top) to carry and store all your paint stuff in, and keep it in good condition.

The paint box

Surprise—it will ALL fit in a box of this size!

You may not believe it, but all of your painting equipment, tools, and supplies will fit in one reasonably small case, box, stack-it container, or mini footlocker. I have an over-size plastic "tackle box." I clean it up carefully after every job and put and keep all my gear here. This way I can be ready to paint in about two minutes, and it's safe from kids, borrowers, the weather, spiders, etc.

(A good painter can even fit a lunch and paint chips in a paint box.)

Getting ready to roll

You've picked the time, place, and color, and have all your equipment and supplies together. Let's do that all-important preparation now!

SURFACE PREPARATION

Before painting, all surfaces must be clean, dry, and free of loose material. Why?

That basic called bonding

Most paint goes on easily and looks great. It can be deceptive, however, because all too often that nice handsome covering is soon flaking, chipping, peeling, or sloughing off. The prime reason is that the paint did not bond—hold tight—to the surface. For example paint will stick like glue to raw brick or unfinished wood, yet the same paint will come off a slick metal surface at first nudge. Do all you can to assure bonding by making sure that:

• The surface is absolutely clean (see following).

• You are using the right paint for the surface in question.

• The atmospheric conditions are right for painting, so the paint doesn't dry too slow or too fast.

Note: If the surface is glossy, it should be deglossed with very fine sandpaper or deglossers.

Cleaning

Paint won't stick to greasy, dirty walls. Dust and lint will also get in the paint and produce a bumpy surface. So at least vacuum before you paint—even nearby areas that won't be painted.

A **dry sponge** is a lifesaver here nearly every time. If the wall is just dusty and grimy, dry sponge it. You can dry sponge a bedroom down in minutes and have it ready to paint. Dry sponges are a special type of super-absorbent soft rubber sponge available at janitorial supply stores and some paint stores. You use them until they're dirt saturated on all sides and then just dispose of them.

Greasy or extra-dirty walls need to be washed, using a good strong cleaner like TSP (or other heavy-duty cleaner). Dilute and apply according to package directions, wearing rubber gloves. Make sure the surface is dry before you paint.

Mildewed surfaces should be cleaned

with a disinfectant cleaner or a 1:5 solution of chlorine bleach/water.

Let the surface dry well after any cleaning operations before applying paint.

After assuring that your target surfaces are good and clean, your indoor preparations otherwise are:

1. Move knickknacks, lamps, pictures, and other vulnerable little things out of the room. Many things that are hard to cover are easy to move.

When painting a room with furniture, we pros generally drop the center ceiling fixture, if any—unscrew it and let it dangle—and trim a generous circle around it. Then we move all the furniture to the middle of the room, cover it well, and just reach over it as necessary with our rollers. This way there is **no more moving** to do!

2. Remove switchplates. This sounds easy, but often when the plates were put back on last time the paint wasn't fully dry, so they're stuck on and have to be chipped and chiseled off. You may have to run a

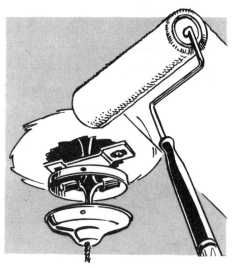

putty knife around under the edges before you can remove the plate. Replace any plates that have seen better days—many pros replace all the switchplates at their own expense because it makes the finished job look so good.

After you remove a plate, put the screws right back in the screw holes of the bare receptacle so you'll be able to find them again.

3. Loosen, *lower, and release* wall and ceiling light fixtures. Clean the fur and flies off and out of them while you're at it. Release or remove any other hardware you can, too.

Watch those chandeliers! Always set something under a chandelier to stake off its territory, so you'll be alerted to walk and work around it instead of into it.

4. Renail protruding nails and countersink them (use a nail set to sink the heads a little below the surface), and fill the resulting holes with spackle.

5. Patch and fill any cracks or holes (see following).

PATCHING HOLES, NICKS, AND CRACKS

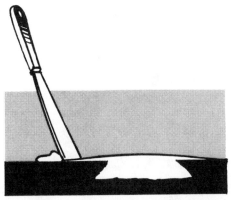

Clean out cracks with the pointed end of a bottle opener, or a screwdriver. Make sure you get any loose material out. Fill with vinyl-type spackling compound, rounded slightly above the surface.

The key here is keeping in mind the fact that paint is only a very thin skin or coating on something, not a filler to hide wall blemishes. If you see an injury or imperfection in something before you paint, don't leave it, assuming an extra-thick coat of paint will cover it. It WON'T. That blemish will reappear, and because everything else is nice and clean and smooth it will only be easier to see. So FIX anything you don't want to be looking at afterward, **before** you paint.

1. Take off—scrape or sand or pry—anything that's loose (or coming loose).

2. Then clean out the crack or hole so that the spackle or filler will be able to reach the surface and adhere to it and hold. Best of all is if you can manage to flare the bottom of the hole out a little. This will really hold the patch in.

3. Use a putty knife to fill the hole with spackle, rounded slightly above the surface to allow for shrinkage, because most spackling shrinks a bit. (You apply and spread spackle with a putty knife just like you butter toast.)

Come back and sand down the rounded spot a little after it dries, to get it flush with the surface. Feeling with your hand is usually the best way to tell if something is smooth or not. Lighting can deceive the eye alone.

Bear in mind that if you sand sheet rock too much, you will injure it and it will "fur out" and won't look good.

4. Most of us get spackle over the whole area around the actual hole—then we wonder what those lumps and bumps are when we paint over it. When you finish filling a hole, take a damp cloth or fine sandpaper and remove all the unnecessary surrounding smears.

5. As for those **hairline cracks**, they seem so innocent and easy to fix with a dab of spackle. Then after the paint is on they seem to reappear quickly. This is because whatever caused them (frost, house shifts, humidity, etc.) will generally recur. For this reason we pros have found that a filler that is flexible and "gives" a little, such as acrylic caulk, is best for

these. Latex caulk works well on long deep cracks, too. Just be sure to wipe away all the excess, and let the caulk dry well, after you fill!

6. For **gaping cracks or giant holes**, use self-adhesive dry wall mesh or joint tape such as Perfatape (it comes in rolls) then spackle over it with sandable spackle. The mesh helps hold the area against shifting and helps prevent recracking.

For other surfaces and problems, ask your paint store. Such service is part of the price of what you buy there.

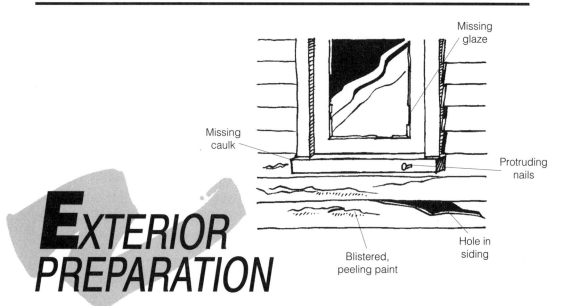

Missing glaze

Missing caulk

Protruding nails

Hole in siding

Blistered, peeling paint

*E*XTERIOR PREPARATION

Cleaning first is important here, too. A rented pressure washer (be sure to follow the instructions that come with it) can have the exterior of a dirty house ready to go in hours.

NEW WOOD must be primed immediately with exterior wood primer. Delaying this important step may mean having to sand to fresh wood. Caulk nail heads and siding joints and around window and door frames. Prime new plywood with latex primer. Top coat with latex house paint.

PREVIOUSLY PAINTED WOOD must be free of loose or peeling paint. Replace loose or missing caulk and window putty. If the surface has problems, correct them before painting.

NEW COMPOSITION BOARD OR HARDBOARD needs the same treatment as new wood. Paint factory-primed siding with oil-based exterior wood primer. Let dry according to label directions and top-coat with latex house paint.

CONCRETE BLOCK must be patched (if necessary), clean, and dry, and all mortar must have cured at least 30 days. Apply latex block filler according to label directions. Top-coat with latex house paint.

POURED CONCRETE, such as basement floors, patios, steps, etc., must cure for at least 30 days before painting. Make sure there are no moisture problems before painting. Etch (roughen) the surface by scrubbing with a mixture of one part muriatic acid to 3 parts water. Wear rubber gloves and long sleeves when applying this. Rinse well with water. The surface should feel like medium grit sandpaper; if not, repeat the etching. Let dry 48-72 hours. Paint with latex or polyurethane floor enamel.

STUCCO should be treated with masonry primer, then allowed to dry. Apply two coats of latex house paint.

ALUMINUM SIDING (for which the claim is often made, "never needs painting") does get painted, on homes and mobile homes, and there is often a problem getting the paint to bond or stick to it. Before attempting to paint aluminum siding, consult the siding manufacturer and your local pro paint store to learn all you can about the best product for your particular type of siding, in your climate.

A sharp stiff chisel or scraper is great for removing flaking or loose paint. A wire brush is fine for light paint peeling or blistering.

Heavy floor sanding paper really cuts through old paint and uneven outside surfaces.

To patch cracks and holes outdoors, use the same principles described on page 19, being sure to use products designed for **exterior** use.

UNDER-COATS AND PRIMERS

Are as sensible as underwear and as important and underrated as the box spring under a mattress.

They look, feel, and smell just like regular paints, but they aren't the same. Undercoats and primers are carefully designed to bridge gaps and to penetrate, smooth, and grip the surface, providing a firm base for the paint to follow.

I've seen four coats of paint over bare wood not cover as well as one coat of good primer. Whenever recommended, and especially on new surfaces of any kind, primer is a smart move. It speeds up the work and helps paint last up to twice as long.

When priming:

❑ If a surface is clean and well painted (even with pretty old paint) it's okay to skip priming.

❑ We pros generally tint primer the color we are going to top coat with, even if that color is a subtle one like gray. This helps a little with coverage and a lot with the scratches that are bound to come later.

❑ Be sure to be generous with it—it is a coating.

❑ Allow plenty of time for primer to dry before applying the paint over it. In damp weather or wet climates this will take longer.

❑ If you find a mark or stain (such as a pen mark) bleeding through even a second coat of primer, use a little shellac over that area only to seal off the stain. Reprime when it dries.

PAINT THINNER

Is inexpensive, so always have plenty of it handy.

Paint thinner is a less volatile form of the solvent mechanics use to clean off greasy parts, and dry cleaners use to clean our clothes. It not only cleans up paint drips, smears, and spills, but reduces the thickness of oil paints and varnishes when needed.

You don't often have to thin paint, because most of it comes just right and generally the thicker it is the better it covers and the longer it lasts. If paint is so thick that it's gluey, however, it'll be hard to apply and usually end up uneven.

USING THINNER

The only real expertise involved here is:

1. Knowing the difference between oil and water-based products, so you always use the right thinner. You need paint thinner for oil-base paints, lacquer thinner for lacquer type paints, and plain old WATER for latex or water base paints.

To make oil paint "work" or flow better, many pros use a product called Pentrol. Adding just a little makes paint flow like oil, while maintaining its hiding and protective qualities.

2. Add thinner sparingly and go slow and easy when thinning paint. Paint does need body to hide imperfections and thickness for endurance. Over-thinned or watery paint is a cinch to put on, but I guarantee you won't like the way it looks when it's dry. Remember: You can always make it thinner if you need to, but you can't thicken it if you get it too thin!

How do you know whether it needs thinning?

Dip a stirring stick into the paint, and if the break point of the drip is about one inch from the end of the stick, your paint is about right.

1"

Beware of Red Hiney Rash
You do some paint cleanup, put the wet thinner rag in your pocket, keep on working… …and end up with a red hiney.

See p. 29 for some other things to keep in mind when working with thinners.

COVERS

The answer to "fear of fallout"

Even the neatest pro will create some drips and drops, or occasionally stumble over a can of paint. But pros are smart enough to prepare and rig for it. They know that every ounce of prevention here means a pound of pleasure at the end of the job, when you're trying to clean up and remove unwelcome paint from surfaces.

One misery of painting you can eliminate immediately is to STOP using

1. newspapers

2. holey old bedspreads and sheets

3. sandwich-wrapper-thin plastic

For covering and protecting your floors and furnishings, these all fight you and con you. They leak, tear, stick to your feet, blow around in the slightest breeze, and hide outlaw paint drips and drops until it's

23

too late—they're dry. You'll spend more time re-covering things after cheap or pinch-hit covers slip off them, or trying to separate and use .00000001 mil sheets of that dry-cleaner-thin plastic, than you will on the whole paint job.

Every home should have not just a bible, but a good 9' x 12' or 12' x 15' painter's cloth dropcloth—preferably canvas. You'll use it again and again and it will last forever. And it won't leak even if you tip the whole paint bucket over on it! You'll find lots of other uses for it, too, and you should be able to get one for under $30, especially if you can manage to get a professional discount.

Rubberized cloth dropcloths are even available now, for greater "clingability."

If you do use plastic to protect middle-of-the-room stuff from roller flecks or spray painting, buy thicker plastic. The thin stuff may catch the paint droplets but they'll chip and drop off all over after they dry, when you're gathering up the plastic. Heavier plastic can be reused, too, and it won't have 40 holes in it before you even get it put down over everything.

HIT THE STRIP!

If you try them, you'll find out why strips (4' x 15' or so) of canvas are another pro painter's secret. We call them "runners" and they're wide enough to protect against fallout and spills, yet easy to handle. We line them up along the walls and keep them kicked up against the baseboard and just move around the room with them. You can also keep your paint containers on them.

Some things we always forget to cover and then fight to clean off later

- our own watch and glasses

(and face and hair)

- railings
- vents
- heaters
- concrete
- shrubs

The shrub solution. Shrubs and trees close up to the side of the house ruin many a paint job (and painter!). You can cover shrubs and trees with a cloth drop-cloth or pull them away with rope—but a piece of plywood is far better. It's fast and impervious and much more comfortable to squeeze up against in tight quarters.

MASKING TAPE

Pros use it a lot, but not where novices do. Novices use it to help assure a neat line on windows and edges, etc. You can generally do that better and faster with a brush only, or a brush and metal edger.

1. We use 2" wide tape mostly, it's best all around.

2. Use it wherever you want to prevent paint penetration.

electrical receptacles and switches

doorknobs and hinges

baseboards (notice we flap the tape here) and the base of immovable fixtures

Instead of using an edger, you can use a strip of tape to hold the carpet away from the baseboard. (When you take it off it cleans the carpet edge, too!)

3. We buy good tape. Cheap tape pleats and tears, and it can't be removed easily.

We pros even slap a couple of strips of tape over the toes of our shoes to keep paint off!

Don't tape off glass windows, unless you are spray-painting. Paint will creep under the tape. If you should lap over a little onto the panes, remember that paint, wet or dry, is easy to remove from glass.

4. You can broaden the "protective strip" wherever you need to by lapping some newspaper onto the tape. Lay the paper down and apply the tape about half on the paper and half on the surface you're protecting.

5. Always press the top edge of the tape

tightly so paint won't bleed through. The worst thing you can have happen in working with masking tape is to have paint creep under it without realizing it. Then you go to take the tape off and discover it's already dry under there—you're dead!

6. Take the tape off while it's still fresh— as soon as the paint is dry, or even while it's still tacky. The longer masking tape stays on, the harder it is to get off, and greater the chance of damaging the surface it's stuck to.

7. Pull it off back over itself.

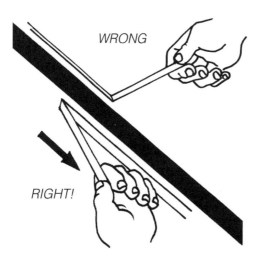

WRONG

RIGHT!

8. After you remove it, gather that used tape together into a ball. Don't drop big long strings of it around—even in the trash they can stick to other things and cause trouble.

DRESS FOR THE MESS

Just as there are swimsuits, fire suits, surgical suits, and even clown suits there are some real advantages to a paint suit— being dressed comfortably, safely, and believe it or not, attractively for painting. It'll boost your morale and make you **feel** like a pro.

Old rags and nice clothes are both the wrong outfit for painting. Remember, as "the painter" you are going to see a lot of action: handling paint, paint tools and thinners, sweating, climbing, carrying things and cleaning. Better be dressed for it!

What does that mean?

Painter's hat: It'll keep paint and falling stuff out of your hair, help keep paint flecks and dribbles out of your eyes and off your glasses. These are nice and light and will stay on your head the whole time, whereas baseball or other caps are like wearing a big cowboy hat in a pickup.

Gloves: Yes, gloves. Especially when you're working outside, they cut down on scrapes and scratches and other injuries, as well as stains and chapping. They

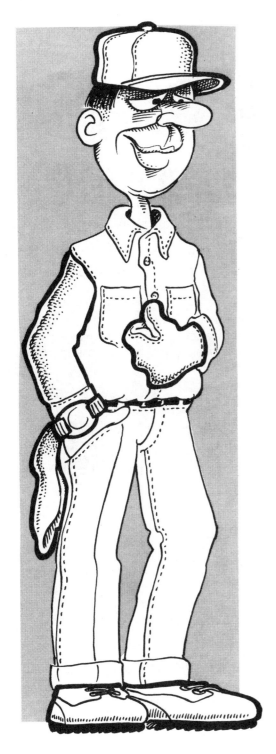

speed the painting process, and cleanup, too.

The light, tight cotton gloves sold for this purpose are okay, but if you want to really get a grip on things, a pair of those cheap light pigskin leather gloves are ideal.

Good gripper shoes: Sure they'll get paint on them, count on it. Save a pair for this purpose and always use them. But wear sturdy good-fitting high traction shoes—old, sad, worn out, slippery "tossers" (especially sandals) will toss you.

Long sleeves: Paint on the arms is guaranteed during any paint job. Why subject your skin to all that thinner? And if you have hairy arms and paint dries on there, bath time will *really* be miserable.

Wear white: White (an old white shirt and pants is fine for this) makes you look and feel like a painter. It'll give you respect and extra help and maybe even a pro discount too, at the paint store.

Turn your watch over: so the face won't get dribbled on—watch backs are easy to clean.

Terry cloth paint rag: Yes, a good paint rag is part of a pro painter's getup. But you don't want a piece of old pillowcase or negligee, cut off jean leg or retired bra. Cotton terry will give you a quick thirsty wipe.

If you don't have a proper paint rag at hand, use some of those good Brawny 100% Recycled paper towels or Scotts paper shop towels. You can even apply stain with them.

ORDER:
The secret of smooth, swift progress

Doing things in the right sequence makes all the difference. It prevents wasted time and motion, confusion, and frustration.

Start by organizing your whole painting operation.

1. Commit to paint, not just in general, but a particular place or thing.

2. Decide **when** you will do it.

3. List the supplies you need, for both painting and preparation.

4. Pick the color and type of paint.

5. Buy your paint and equipment.

6. Prep the room or area.

7. Prep yourself.

8. PAINT (doing each part of the job in the right order).

9. Clean up.

10. Store your equipment and any leftover materials.

*D*oing it!

Order to paint a room in

Start at the top and work your way down.

1. Ceiling Paint a wide strip all around the edges of the ceiling, where it meets the wall. Use a ladder or roller with extension handle to do the rest of the ceiling. Start in a corner and work your way across the short side to maintain a wet edge. (See p. 38.)

2. Walls Paint a wide strip along the ceiling, floor, and woodwork with a brush. Use a roller for the rest, coming as close to the edges as possible to create a clean, uniform appearance.

3. Woodwork Paint all trim around doors, windows, ceilings, and floor. On woodwork and other trim do the edges first, then horizontal sections.

Trim or "cut in" all the edges first so you can lap over them with a roller and the trimming line won't show.

4. Doors Paint decorative panels first, then flat areas in between. Work from the top of the door down. Do the edges, top, and bottom before the face and back of the door. I always do the frame and casing after the door itself.

5. Windows Paint them from the center out, and top to bottom. Inside first, then out.

6. Floors Start in a corner diagonally opposite the room exit. Use a brush to cut in the edges, then use a wide (4-inch) brush or a roller with an extension handle.

P.S. When two people are painting together, one generally trims and the other keeps things covered and rolls. If the trimmer is right handed, they work to the left, so they're reaching in front of themselves, and can see their work better. And this keeps the trimmer out of the way of the roller person.

PAINT SAFE

It saves cussing and hospital confinements, as well as YOU!

More people die of disgust or are wounded emotionally when painting than are hurt physically in the process. But there's no reason to have any kind of pain involved in your painting.

A quick check of the following will preserve you as well as your target surfaces.

❑ Always read labels and follow manufacturer's suggestions, to prevent toxic contact with anything you're using.

❑ Always keep and store paint and thinners well away from the little ones.

HERE'S HOW THE LIVING ROOM TURNED OUT, LEROY.

- Keep your paint and thinners away from sparks or flames, too, and make the painting area a No Smoking one. NEVER use gasoline for thinner or cleanup.
- Keep doors and windows open when you're painting, especially when using oil or solvent-thinned paints. If you ever start to feel dizzy or nauseous while painting, stop immediately and get some fresh air.
- If paint gets into your eyes, or into a wound or sore, rinse it out immediately with water. If irritation persists after flushing the area for 15 minutes, consult a doctor.
- Paint splatters on skin and hair come off easiest while they're still wet. Wipe splatters with the right solvent for that type of paint, and follow immediately with a soap and water wash. Be careful here because some solvent thinners can irritate sensitive skin. When painting, always cover your hair and as much skin as possible. See p. 26.
- Don't ever spray paint without a mask.
- Dispose of used paint rags immediately in a garbage can outside—never store them. Thinner- or paint-soaked rags should be dropped in a bucket of water if for some reason you can't set them outside immediately.
- Working and reaching around electrical lines or outlets can be an electrifying experience—be careful. Paint is a liquid and a good conductor of electricity, as is the metal frame of a roller or an extension pole.
- Especially if you are afraid of heights, be sure to stay within your comfort limits when working in high places. Read the next page ten times, and you'll live to paint again and again.

RE**A**CHING THE HEIGHTS

(The right way to do it)

Some painting jobs only take about two minutes, but it takes two hours and two twenty-dollar rentals to get at them. What we need is **ACCESS**. Quick, safe, access to a paintable surface is the single biggest secret of pro painters. Here's how you can do it just like we do.

Stepladder
(aluminum, wood, or fiberglass)

Buy a heavy duty model, you'll never regret it. A 5-footer is best for inside work and a 7-footer for outside work.

Be sure the lock hinges are locked before you step on there.

Never move a ladder when there's paint on the stand.

Extension ladder

(aluminum, wood, or fiberglass)

These are two straight ladders connected together in such a way that they will extend out into one longer one.

14-foot is the best size. You can take it apart to make two handy-size ladders.

Pad the top of an extension ladder with a towel or a rubber "ladder boot," so it won't dig and scratch the surface it's leaning against.

Always have your ladder at a safe angle.

This means one foot out for every four feet up.

An extension ladder can be used on a roof perfectly. Just take one half of the ladder out and clip the slide hooks on the end over the peak of the roof.

"A" Frame

You could call these "hinged extension ladders," and I love them. You can work on them from either side and also use them as a plank platform.

Ten-footers are great, and if you have a big place they are well worth owning.

12'

3'

PUT YOUR NAME ON ALL YOUR LADDERS
(they'll be less likely to walk away)

Your best reaching tool, an

Extension handle

USE IT, USE IT! You'll be able to cover eight times the area with half the effort and zero climbing. A good painter's extension handle can shrink down to two feet for close-in painting, and extend out with a click to four feet. The length of the handle should fit your height and the size of your painting reach.

The plank

A pro won't paint homes without it!

A plank like this is simply a portable painting platform that reduces the mileage you have to cover when you paint. It can be an 8-foot (or all the way up to a 12-foot) 2 X 12, or a professional aluminum plank. There are even extension planks available that adjust from 8 to 12 feet.

A plank gives you incredible advantage—look at the following setups and think of the climbing-up-and-down time you save. On a plank you can walk around up high, and keep your paint bucket right there with you if you want to.

Redwood makes the perfect home plank. Whatever kind you use, make sure it's a sound, sturdy one.

Bevel the ends a little.  Paint the ends red (to help keep you aware of where they are), but do not paint the entire plank or it will be slippery.

You can leave your materials on the ground if you're using an extension handle from a plank—even dip and refill your roller right from on high!

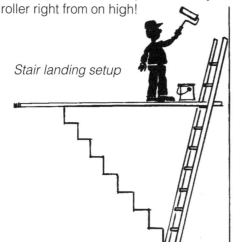

Stair landing setup

Over furniture

See what a nice big work area it gives you, for painting, papering, or cleaning.

Planks are safe, fast, and inexpensive. Just don't get so enthusiastic that you walk off the end—it'll bring an abrupt end to your painting day! I always set something big and harmless on the plank, like a plastic bucket, to warn me of the approaching end.

SCAFFOLDING

Isn't just for big contractors. For the most part it's easily rented, and if you use it enough, it's not a bad idea to own one. Scaffolding offers something ladders and planks don't—a large, floor-like working area, and if the job of preparation is going to be extensive with lots of sanding and patching, and then several coats of paint, then scaffolding is a good idea. Hardware stores and many paint stores now have home size small scaffolds that really work and can be folded up when not in use. Start noticing and looking at scaffolding. You'll get some ideas that save you time, effort, and money.

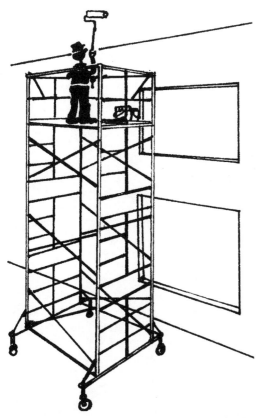

When I set up scaffolding or planks and ladders in a difficult place, and two coats of paint are needed, I leave the scaffolding up and go do something else while the first coat is drying. Then I put on the second coat before I move the scaffolding. Saves time and stress and damage from moving and setting up.

> *Never stand on a plastic bucket. We all have empty 5-gallon paint buckets and we all get in a hurry, or are too lazy to fetch the ladder for a short reach. Don't do it, or someday you'll be surprised to have one collapse right under you.*

THE PRO WAY TO PAINT

Relax now... you only have to learn how to paint once, because some skills are basic to all painting.

First, read

The manufacturer's directions for applying the paint and the drying time it calls for.

Now look and listen

Is it too windy? Raining? Too hot? You always want to avoid painting in direct sunlight. If a hot sun causes too rapid drying of the paint, heat blistering may result. This traps solvents under a surface film, where they vaporize and put pressure against the topcoat. This is most common with dark paints, which are naturally heat absorbent.

If the time you picked turns out to be a bad one, reschedule.

The lid

The lid, itself, off a quart, gallon, or 5-gallon container of paint will hold at least a half gallon of paint. (At least that's what you'll swear when you step on it!) The Lord never created a spot on this earth for wet paint lids, and they can and will throw a job into overtime, if you let them.

So after you shake and stir the can, right at the start, take your brush and clean that lid off. There's lots of good paint there. Then set the lid, face up, on top of something (not on the floor!) to dry while you paint for real.

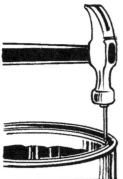

Punching a hole in the inside lip gutter of the can will eliminate "can run."

Mix!

Make sure the paint is thoroughly mixed. Always have the paint store shake it on their machine, and then stir it again yourself if it sits for long before you use it.

You can shake paint to mix it, but not varnish. Always stir varnish—it will foam and be full of bubbles if you shake it.

When you're using stains, keep stirring and stirring and stirring! Stir not just before but *during* the job. Paint won't settle in that short a time, but stain will. If you don't stir it every so often while you're working with it, the solids and pigment will settle to the bottom and the oil will stay on top, and soon you'll have two colors and poor coverage,

If two mixed cans of the same type of paint appear to be somewhat different in shade (they're both supposed to be Plan-

tation Pink, but they look a little different), mix them both together well before you start.

Ventilate!

For some reason most people think that heat is what's needed to dry things. Wrong! It's air circulation that does most of the drying. Even cool air that is circulating freely will dry paint faster than a sealed up house with the heat turned to 80 degrees. Breathing paint fumes reduces your mental and physical efficiency, too. Get plenty of air flow—it'll help you *and* the paint.

NOW LET'S CUT DRIPS BEFORE WE START

Most drips and slops of paint come from overload, or trying to carry too much paint on the tool. Professional brushes and rollers hold much more paint, so even when the excess is brushed or rolled off before you start, there's still plenty on there. Your goal now is to get that loaded tool to your work surface as quickly as you can. Even the thickest paint may be slow to drip or run, but it won't hang on a brush or roller forever.

Where you set your paint container makes a difference here. You shouldn't have to walk back and forth from it to your work surface—you want it within "pivot" range. About 4 feet away is best—so you won't knock it over when you swing your arm, and you won't kick it over. But you won't have to walk or reach far for it either.

When brushing

Dip the bristles no more than halfway into the paint, and then holding the brush flat, wipe the back side and the bottom of the brush against the bucket rim before you start.

When rolling

To fill your roller, set it on the screen and roll your way into the paint, until two or three sides are well saturated. Never dip the roller deeper than the roller axle! Then roll the excess off on the screen, so your roller will hold plenty of paint without dripping.

Keep a sharp eye out for runs as you paint along, so you can roll or brush them away before they harden. A couple of places you always have to watch is around the corner (when you *roll* corners, especially), and down the other side, when you paint the edge or top of a door, etc.

BASIC BRUSH TECHNIQUE

To avoid brush marks, always end up the painting of an area by brushing back toward the area already painted.

Angle your brush to do sashes.

Most pros hold a trim or sash brush just like you hold a pencil, at that familiar-feeling 45-degree angle. Then with a simple bend of the wrist we can paint horizontally or vertically.

Most moves with a brush should come natural and follow what feels comfortable. Just remember your paintbrush is an artist's tool, not a war club or means of getting even with those kitchen or bathroom walls!

Painting right up against another surface—ceiling, woodwork, floor, fixture, etc.—that isn't supposed to be painted is the downfall of the average amateur painter. Cover such things whenever you can (see p. 23), or use an edger. And bear in mind, at all times, this important dab of brush wisdom: It is better to be 1/8 of an inch short of the edge you are trimming, than 1/1000th of an inch over onto it!

So keep those bristles at least 1/8-inch away!

Never work out of a full gallon or 5-gallon can. You increase your chances of dunking the bristles too deeply into the paint, creating a mess. A full container is heavy and awkward to move around, plus you risk a truly major spill.

A small container like a quart can of paint, on the other hand, is too small to work from with a 2 1/2-inch sash brush.

The bristles will catch on the edge of the can and flip paint all over.

A gallon can, no more than half or a third full is best.

When moving around to paint or trim, I keep the paint can in my hand. If I'm at a window for a while or doing something else intricate and time-consuming, I set the can up on something about waist high.

You can also set your paint supply into a large shallow plastic or cardboard container, and move it around with you and work from it. This catches drips and protects against spills and is easy to clean up (or just toss) afterward.

THE RIGHT WAY TO ROLL

When rolling, go over every surface three or more times, in the pattern shown here.

Rolling out of a bucket and screen combination is 600% better than out of a roller pan—remember that!

Dip the roller in the bucket, roll off the excess paint on the screen, then start applying.

When the roller is getting empty (it feels light and it isn't covering), dip it again.

Always roll in an up and down pattern. You go UP on the first stroke so paint won't puddle down.

A roller won't get every tiny bit of the surface with one roll. You need to go over everything three or more times for a good looking, well distributed paint job. The first roller pass may appear adequate, but small "pinholes" or air holes are there that won't show until the paint is dry.

Because the roller has a lot more paint on it right after you've dipped, and basically you want to spread it over a 4 or 5 square foot area, the first few strokes should be done in a "W" pattern, or a series of "V's." Then go back to where you started and roll up and down over the same area 3 or 4 times.

On the last stroke, always go the same way—the pattern of up and down rolling is a little different, and when the light hits it later it will be noticeable. Doing all your finish strokes in the same direction is like brushing velvet or some other napped fabric. You have to make all your strokes in the same direction, because any in the opposite direction will reflect light differently and make the surface look streaky. If you remember this rule you'll have a beautiful even surface for no extra effort.

When painting walls or ceilings with a roller, cut in the corners and edges first with a brush. Then you won't have to go so close to the edge when you start working with the roller. This reduces the chances of rolling over onto the adjacent wall and helps insure a clean, finished look.

Once the trimming is done, paint the ceiling, and then the walls.

Create a clean edge. When painted walls butt up to a textured ceiling, scrape off the little nubs right next to the wall with a screwdriver.

All rollers create somewhat of an orange peel effect. If you don't like this, you can roll the paint on, and then brush the surface lightly behind the roller.

Textured walls are the most forgiving to paint. They usually look presentable even after a poor rolling job.

Trimming the fuzzy edges of the roller will help minimize roller lines.

Whether brushing or rolling

- Work in 4 to 5 foot wide vertical stripes, and always work from painted to unpainted areas.

- The big edge in painting is—**the wet edge.** Move across the wall, top to bottom, always working from the wet edge. This will assure a smooth and seamless finish. For example, if you stop for lunch halfway, the paint has a chance to dry. When you  come back to it, you overlap the "dry" edge and this portion gets two coats. And this "stripe" will be noticeable. If you work from a "wet" edge the whole wall gets the same coating. When you have to stop and start, do it at the corners or the end of wall sections.

- If some emergency comes along during the job and you have to leave, the paint will begin to dry. On the wall it won't really hurt anything, but some of your tools can crust over. If you're using a bucket and roller you can simply set the roller down in the bucket, suspended out of the paint by its handle (that's what the clip on the handle of a pro roller is for). Then your brush(es) can be nestled between the roller and the screen. Cover the top of the container with a damp cloth. Paint can stay hours and hours like this without setting up.

- **Don't over-paint!** When you do that, the sharp, crisp edges of corners and trim become so gobbed they make the place look cheap and sloppy (and you can hardly tell the trim from the wall). Any damage to the surface, which happens in even the best-kept homes, is deep and ugly and almost impossible to blend in when the surface is repainted.

- On the other hand, **don't skimp** on the paint. Trying to see how little you

can get by with will leave you with a job that looks bad and will have to be redone too soon. Put on enough paint to flow easily. You'll catch the rhythm of this after you're into the job.

- When doing a 2-coat job, always cover on the first coat as perfectly as you can. Too often we know we're going to paint something again, so we don't worry about any missed spots. We never cover on any coat as well as we imagine, so be most careful on that first coat!

- If coverage is a concern and you know you can only paint something once, after you come to the end of the wall, go back to where you started—where your first application has begun to slightly dry—and take the extra time to lightly go over the whole wall.

- I always look over the whole job carefully after the first coat dries, so I can catch and sand down any drips, excess spackle I accidentally  painted over, lint or hair, etc., caught in the first coat.

- You apply a second coat just like the first, and it's faster because there's little or no prepping and no additional covering to be done. If the sheetrock job was poor and some seams or uneven places still show after your second coat, this is a construction not a painting problem and it isn't going to go away. Remember, any fixing you want to do has to be done **before** you paint.

DOOR AND WINDOW WISDOM

Don't forget the doors!

Doors get used and abused more than just about any other part or surface in a building, yet in painting as well as cleaning they get overlooked or skipped. Often just doing up all the doors nicely would look as good as redoing the whole place.

You do doors like anything else, except they usually take a little more sanding and preparation (because they have so many nicks, marks, scuffs, and scratches). Prepare them well, then clean them down good with a good strong cleaning solution maybe even a light, light sanding. Doors, more than any part

39

of the house, need good bonding of the newly applied product.

Doors don't look so great with that stippled roller texture, but I roll my doors anyway and then brush behind the roller for a "sprayed" look. I seldom take doors off to paint them—I just put down drop-cloths and tape the hardware.

Panes don't have to be a pain

Windows, ugh, groan. All those edges, all those sides, all those little ledges and tracks and crevices. And they're always so dirty and full of moth bodies and loose caulk. They're often hard to get to, and hard to reach all parts of. They have an inside AND outside that has to be done, too. Because they're a working mecha-nism, you can't paint all parts at once and if you're not careful, you'll end up painting them shut.

A life saver here is an angled trim brush so you can cut a straight edge. A time-saver you'll appreciate, especially if you're doing a lot of windows, is a product called Wagner Glass Mask. It's a waxy film you smear right on the edge of the glass that makes paint come off easily with a razor blade.

On outside windows with dry peeling paint, completely scrape off the old paint and fill splits and cracks with wood filler. Start with a coat of good alkyd (oil base) primer. It will penetrate the wood, whereas latex just coats it. Finish with two coats of oil base paint, the glossier, the better to repel water. Inside or out, when you're finished sanding and scraping, vacuum or brush up all the loose stuff everywhere including last season's collection of dead insects, spider webs, and loosened bird

For fast painting around panes: Press the tip of the brush in one corner and pull it across to the next.

poop. If the tracks or sills, etc. are really grimy, wash them first and let them dry well before you prime.

Paint wooden window tracks only if they are peeling, otherwise buildup will gum up the works. Never paint aluminum tracks—they don't need it.

WHEN YOU'RE PAINTING OUTSIDE

• Start on a shaded side and never work in direct sun.

• If you're using alkyd or oil products, check that all dew has evaporated before you start.

• As you begin each section, arrange your dropcloths to shield fixtures, railings, steps, flower beds, and the like.

SPRAY PAINTING

It looks so fast, so easy, on TV and watching the pros do it. But 95% of the time when ordinary people try it, the National Guard has to be called in before they're through. (I painted 300 cars once, inadvertently, while doing one roof!)

Spray painting is fast and easy IF:

• You have lots of easily accessible footage to paint.

• You have a high quality gun and any necessary scaffolding.

You can rent a nice airless unit, fairly trouble free, for about $40 a day. You'll have less overspray with an airless sprayer, because you aren't spraying a mixture of paint and air, but 100% pure paint.

Your "watch outs" here are:

1. Keeping fallout—drift and overspray—to a minimum. In this kind of painting it's ESPECIALLY important to cover up anything you don't want painted. Be extra careful outdoors, where with the slightest breeze paint can easily drift onto other people's property. Don't spray on windy days, or around corners.

2. Keeping the paint perfectly clean—even a mosquito eyebrow in there will plug the nozzle. Paint stores have filters that will help out here. With spray paint you need to be especially sure to follow the manufacturer's mixing and thinning directions.

3. Make sure the area is well ventilated. And wear a respirator and/or safety glasses if you need to.

4. Remember that pressure! Airless spray guns are wonderful and they work well without air because the paint or whatever is in there is under 1500-3000 pounds of pressure from a highly efficient pump. This shoots out a stream of paint like a needle, so never point the gun at anyone, including yourself (don't look at it while it's running to see if the nozzle is clear, for instance). Never leave the gun sitting anywhere while the machine is on. Guns of any kind are always an attraction for kids and they will pick them up to play with them. A spray machine like this can maintain a dangerous amount of pressure even when it's off, so always release or bleed off the pressure before leaving the gun anywhere.

Wear a stocking cap and rub a little Vaseline on your face before you start. It protects you and makes cleaning the paint up and off a LOT easier.

MASTERING THE BASIC SPRAY STROKE

This means keeping the nozzle about eight inches away from what you're painting, and never swinging or fanning the gun while spraying. That will guarantee an uneven coat. Keep the nozzle at a 90 degree angle to the surface at all times—firm wrist control is the secret here.

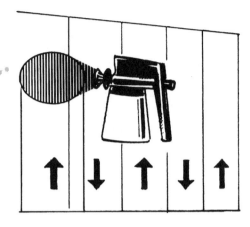

Keep the gun in constant motion and overlap each stroke a few inches. Your goal is to apply a thin, even coat so the paint doesn't pile up anywhere and run.

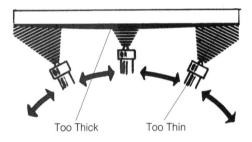

Too Thick   Too Thin

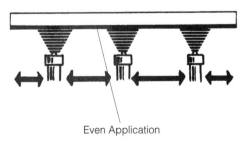

Even Application

You can use a shield to cut in windows and edges.

Don't laugh, this has happened many times to most of us, not just the Three Stooges.

SPILLS

How to prevent and survive them

Painting, like eating, generates a lot of overflow—slops, dribbles, speckles, drips, drops, overspray, and spills. Not to mention big-time pan and bucket accidents. Calamities do lessen as you gain experience. But in the meantime, here's how to defuse disaster.

The golden rule of paint removal

There is no "later" with paint. How soon you remove it has everything to do with how hard it is to get rid of it.

Immediately = Easy
Later = You better like the color!

Roller flecks

Fresh: Wipe with an absorbent cloth dampened with solvent or water, depending on the type of paint, and then polish the area clean with another, fresh cloth.

Old: Wet a white-nylon faced sponge with the appropriate solvent (thinner or water) and scrub gently to loosen and remove.

Old, stubborn: Wet the surface with water or the appropriate solvent, and scrape gently with a putty knife.

Overlap or misguided stroke

Dampen a cloth with thinner and rub the area gently, or go after it with a cloth-covered finger.

Passing pet or person

(Clothes, skin, fur, or equipment picks up some paint). Wipe with solvent-moistened cloth, then (especially if it's skin or fur) rinse or wipe well with water.

Whole can (tanker) spill

Use a squeegee and dustpan, or thin pieces of cardboard, to get the bulk of it up and back into a bucket. (So you can strain and reclaim or dispose of it later.)

Then use a cotton terry cloth to blot up all of the remaining paint possible, and finish up by blotting with a cloth dampened with the appropriate solvent, until no more paint appears on a clean cloth.

PAINT PROBLEMS

If you do all of the simple things I've talked about so far, you'll have few if any of these. The following are the most common and what to do about them.

Holiday A place (in brushed, rolled, or sprayed-on paint) where the paint doesn't cover. You simply missed that spot, or there weren't enough passes over the area, so the paint is too thin there. Lightly recover it, feathering the edges to blend with the surrounding paint.

Sag A little too much paint was put on, and the surface couldn't hold it, so it sagged. Just lightly rebrush or reroll the area before it dries, or while it's still tacky.

Run A lot too much paint was applied—you've created a little paint river, and you might have to rag it all off and start over, if you can't manage to brush or roll it back into the corral. Keep your eyes open for runs as you work, so you won't have to sand them off later, after they've dried.

Orange peeling The paint in that spot is heavily textured, because it didn't adhere to the surface properly and/or was applied too heavily.

Rebrush or re-roll the spot before it dries to flatten it.

Bleeding pool Paint won't hold or flatten properly on the surface—the surface just sucks it in. The answer here is to apply one coat and

let it dry a little. Then a heavy second, or even third coat if necessary, will cover it. Shellacking or heavily priming extra-absorbent spots before you paint will usually prevent this problem.

Alligatoring A second coat was applied over an incompatible paint, or over a still-wet first coat. So the second coat didn't form a bond with the surface. To remedy this

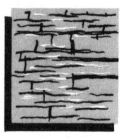

you have to remove everything down to the bare surface and repaint, making sure that the first coat dries thoroughly and doesn't contain too much oil.

Slow drying The climate, the weather, painting too thickly, using an incompatible thinner, or a combination of all of these can cause the paint to dry very slowly. More air circulation and patience… patience… patience is the answer.

Old marks bleeding through It means the marks have solvents in them that your primer and paint aren't able to seal off. After the present coat of paint dries, let the area dry well, and then recoat it with paint.

Paint failure The paint is just plain too hard to work with. It's too hot or too cold. Reread p. 4.

Finishing up

There are still a few things to be done, but they're almost a pleasure because they are the little touches that will really show off your finished job!

Now is the time to walk back past all of the work, and admire it. Any flaws? Now is the time to get them.

Save some touchup paint in a small container with a tight-fitting lid. And no matter what you put it in, mark it (you'll forget what it is for sure if you don't). A dab of the paint itself on the top of the lid will do it!

While the paint is still tacky, move the sash and sills apart a couple of times on old windows so the paint won't glue them shut.

What about those last little defects you only see when the whole job is done? That dried paint dribble, the skip or thin spot you didn't see till now, the bug, or piece of hair, lint, or paintbrush bristle stuck in that otherwise pristine surface? Or the gouge you made when you moved the table back in place?

If you do see a few little things that need attention, be sure to let the paint dry first before you try to fix them. If it's still wet (even if it appears dry to the touch), you'll make a mess if you try to perform any repair operations on it. So let it dry and then come back and sand and fill or whatever, and then touch up the paint, blending or "feathering" the edges as you do.

> *Just as you finish painting that wall perfectly, one tiny little mosquito lights on the surface and sticks there. This really irks you, so with a fumbling thumb and index finger you pinch and maul and pulverize until you have a 2-inch mar on the wall—the bloody, dismembered mosquito. Had you merely cast a jaundiced eye at the little buzzer and left him to his fate until the paint dried, you could have brushed the microscopic cadaver off without a mark.*

Put the switchplates and outlet covers and light fixtures back. Be sure the paint is good and dry before you do this, too.

Seek out and dispose of all paint rags, paint-loaded paper towels, almost-empty paint cans, lids, etc.

Unshroud everything, remove the dropcloths and shake them out well and put them away.

 Take the masking tape off everything, and don't forget to roll it into a ball before you toss it!

 Clean the inevitable smudges and speckles off windows, the ladder, your watch, etc., while they're still fresh and easy to remove. And get the paint off all the things you didn't protect (because you said "Surely it won't hit *that!*").

 Move furniture back into place. Replace knickknacks, pictures, etc., before they get damaged wherever you crammed them.

 Vacuum up the paint droplets that fell off any plastic dropcloths, any caulk or spackle blobs, etc.

 After you've finished painting the outside of the house, move any sprinklers well away from the siding, to avoid ending up with those ugly grey circles on your nice new paint job. No need to water your house, it won't grow!

 Put your paint clothes in to wash if they need it. Change into clean clothes and get the paint off your face and hands and body before you pat yourself on the back and everyone starts hugging you for what a great job you've done.

CLEANUP:

Doesn't have to get you down

I know it comes at a bad time. It's late, we're exhausted from the whole painting effort, and all we want is to have a cold orange juice and sit back and admire our freshly finished job.

You don't need to dread cleanup, though. Done right, it goes fast and easy. If you've followed all the instructions in this book up to this point, there'll be very little cleanup to do. Your covers caught the paint, your clothes kept it off you, and pro tools are designed to clean quickly. It's almost exhilarating!

1. Move yourself and the equipment away from the newly painted area and any furnishings so you won't rub, spill, or splash anything on them. Spread your dropcloth.

2. A roller can contain several cups of paint and it will keep coming out forever. So always scrape them with the groove in the handle of the paint stick before you start rinsing or applying thinner.

3. Then smack the roller screen down on top of the 5-gallon container to shake the paint out of it and into the bucket.

4. Pour any leftover paint back into the original can and remove the bulk of the remaining paint from the sides of the bucket with your brush, wiping it back into the original can. Then put the lid back on the paint can and set your brush on top of it.

5. Put the roller screen back into your 5-gallon bucket and add water or thinner.

6. Then slosh the roller enthusiastically up and down in the cleaning liquid. This will penetrate and loosen the remaining paint. Change the water or thinner as needed and repeat.

7. When and if you can spin the roller on something like a railing outside, it will help flip the water out fast. Another old pro cleanup secret is to aim a high pressure hose at the side of the roller and in seconds it will whirl itself clean as it spins like a fast wheel.

8. Now the brush. As soon as I finish the final rinse of the roller, I dip my brush into a bucket of thinner or water and agitate it up and down and around. Remember paint holds in the roots of a brush, so you can't just give it a quick dip to get it clean. Then I spin the brush, or tap it on the toe of my shoe to flip the moisture out.

9. Turn the 5-gallon bucket upside down and set the screen on top to dry. Remove the roller cover from the frame to speed its drying, too.

I always rinse once more after the brush or roller looks clean. You can tell "clean" by the amount of color still coming out of the tool.

I always hang my brushes after cleaning, or lay them flat, so the bristles will keep their shape as they dry, and be all ready to go again.

For long storage, add a little cooking oil to the bristles and wrap the brush in aluminum foil. If you're using the brush for latex paints, wash the oil out with dish detergent, then rinse well, before your next painting session.

Never freeze a paint brush!

P.S. Unless that old stiff brush is a real expensive one, resuscitation isn't usually worth the effort.

> *Clean brushes stay soft, and they don't shed particles into, or otherwise pollute, your nice new paint!*

LEFTOVERS:

Don't just dump 'em

Painting, like most things, is not neutral when it comes to impact on the environment—it either helps or hurts it. Any hurt in these days of safer paints comes primarily from what we do with the leftovers. Paint costs a lot to buy, and if you don't handle it right it costs a lot to have left over.

Most states do not allow liquid paint in landfills. So your choices here are:

1. If it's just a little, I'd roll the rest of it right on the wall or whatever. Give it another, or a heavier coat. This will not only give the surface a longer life, but keep the paint a positive.

2. If too much to use this way is left over, make sure the lid fits tight and keep the can somewhere it won't freeze. Then when some little job comes up, or you come across some surface you want to clean up and protect (and the color doesn't really matter), use it. You can even mix it up together with the other leftovers, if they're the same type of paint), and apply it ALL! (Even if that means four coats.)

Spread on, and protecting some surface is the best place for old paint.

3. Find someone else who will use it NOW—neighbor, family member, school, theater group, etc.

4. If you must discard latex paint, leave the lid off so it dries up first, and so your local waste collector can see it is hard and dry.

Or paint that old paint onto a big absorbent piece of cardboard or other waste material, and after it dries, dispose of that.

5. Enamel/epoxy/oil paints that must be discarded are toxic waste. Hold them in some place safe from kids and sparks or flame until toxic waste collection day.

6. Paint thinner and brush cleaner can be used over and over if you let them "settle out" and drain the clean/clear thinner off the top. (And label what you put it in, so you remember!)

REMEMBER!!

- Never dump paint (of any kind) down drains or storm sewers.

- Empty aerosols explode when burned!

- Used paint rags can catch fire by spontaneous combustion (and burn the whole place down).

Now you're ready to clip out the Painting Ready List on the next page and get started!

PAINTING **READY** LIST

❑ Date _____

❑ Color (name and #)_____

❑ Location _____

❑ Help _____

❑ Transportation _____
    (do you have a way to haul whatever you'll be picking up?)

❑ Money _____
    (don't forget your wallet or checkbook)

❑ Paint (plenty!)	❑ Roller frame
❑ Paint paddles	❑ Roller covers
❑ Thinner	❑ 5-gallon bucket
❑ Good (cloth) dropcloths	❑ Roller screen
❑ Paint rags/cloths	❑ Extension handle
❑ Masking tape	❑ Ladder
❑ Sandpaper	❑ Painting clothes
❑ Spackling	❑ _____
❑ Putty knife	❑ _____
❑ Brushes	❑ _____

 *quick refresher now*

DO

- Remove all pets and kids from the scene before you start.
- Paint early in the day whenever you can.
- Ventilate your work area well.
- Dress for the mess.
- Use professional tools rather than gizmos and gadgets.
- Buy enough paint to avoid running out.
- Read the label before you start, maybe even the day before.
- Stir and mix any paint or varnish well before using it (this is best done by the store).
- Prepare well before you paint.
- PREVENT paint from getting on things it's not supposed to by using good sense, good masking tape, good covers, good paint, and good equipment—drips will be cut way down with this combination.
- Get spills and spatters of paint off IMMEDIATELY.
- Work off a wet edge.
- Let paint dry well between coats, and after the final coat, before you start moving stuff back in place.

DON'T

- Paint when the weather conditions are against you.
- Paint something if it doesn't need it. If you can make it look good by just cleaning it, clean it.
- Get help from a friend or relative who hates to paint, but did help his mother/cousin once.
- Ever pay a pro (or any painter) in advance.
- Put your faith in "wet paint" signs, they're the least believed (and most tempting to test) warnings in the world.
- Expect paint to fill holes or repair the wall.
- Skip priming if it's needed.
- Over paint. Too much paint will only chip off and look ugly.
- Go too close to any surface you're supposed to stay off of. Keep your brush back an 1/8 of an inch from it—no one will notice.
- Use makeshift ways to reach the heights.
- Move a ladder with paint on it, you'll lose every time!
- Put off cleanup!!

About the Author

For more than 38 years now, the easiest way to identify Don Aslett has been by the paint somewhere on him—his hands, clothes, shoes, eyelids, and even on his wallet!

During his second year of college he started his now multi-million-dollar cleaning company. From the day he learned how to paint from a professional painter who was one of his first employees, painting faster and better became a passion. Paint contracting was soon a division of Don's corporation, and for more than three decades now he has been out there on the job, painting houses and condominiums, commercial buildings and churches, inside and out.

As Don did ever more media appearances across the country in connection with his best-selling books, he found that his audiences were passionately interested in painting, too. Everyone has to do it, and everyone wanted to know "the pro secrets of painting"—how to do it faster and easier with better results.

Don put together a presentation for home and garden shows on the subject, but people clamored for written material to take away with them. Paint company brochures didn't have enough, most books had too much. So Don called six of the best pro painters together and pooled his thoughts with theirs to prepare this guide to the real basics of professional-quality painting—the things you most need to know to paint well, fast, and inexpensively (and to enjoy it, too!).

Don owns and operates several businesses, he is a television and radio personality, and the author of more than thirty books on cleaning and business. He and his wife Barbara live on a ranch in Southern Idaho, and have six children and now seventeen grandchildren.

Other Aslett books for the professional cleaner you won't want to miss...

Cleaning up is big business, a $35+ billion dollar industry. It's a growing industry, one that offers good income and a secure future to those who can do and manage the work effectively and have the will to succeed.

Cleaning is also one of the easiest fields to enter. It requires very little start-up capital, yields an amazing 30% average return on investment, and offers the kind of life that will satisfy the dreams and needs of many who have been thinking of starting a business of their own: freedom of choice, attractive income potential, no special educational requirements, tax advantages, opportunities everywhere, and the chance to branch out into numerous related careers.

If you want to investigate one of the many exciting specialties in the profession or explore the whole constellation of cleaning industry opportunities. *Cleaning Up For a Living* is the book you want. I will ensure that whatever branch of the business you choose turns out a success.

Cleaning Up For a Living is a complete, comprehensive, step-by-step guide to everything you'll ever need to know about the business. It's written in a down-to-earth, lively style that makes even the most "technical" subject easy to grasp and understand, and includes 34 pages of forms of all kinds you can just copy and use.

208 pages, illustrated; $16.99.

The most comprehensive training manual ever for the frontline cleaner. You will learn here, from a master, not merely how to clean, but all the hidden and equally important "people" skills.

Don Aslett founded Varsity Contractors, Inc., a total facility maintenance firm, forty years ago. The wisdom and knowledge of Don and all of his Varsity managers, supervisors, and cleaning crews is boiled down here in *The Professional Cleaner's Personal Handbook.*

The first half of the book provides all of the important background information every cleaner needs. It begins by putting the cleaning profession into perspective, explaining the position of pride and responsibility it unquestionably is. Among the many topics it goes on from there to cover are: safety, how to care for your equipment, professional ethics, how to get clients and coworkers to like you, how to avoid the pitfalls and cope with the doldrums of the cleaning career, how to assess your own performance, how to handle the wide, wild world of "what ifs" (unexpected, unusual, and "emergency" things) that crop up every day and week, and how to further your career in cleaning. The second half of the book is the actual "how-to" of cleaning, including how to organize yourself and your crew.

200 pages; illustrated; $10.00.

Folder of over 300 easy-to-reproduce line drawings, from Don Aslett's own cartoonist. They'll bring life to your newsletters, flyers, cards, or brochures, anywhere you want or need a graphic depicting the greatest profession on earth. Not available on computer disk.

25 pages of illustrations; $19.95

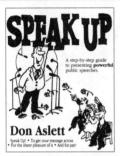

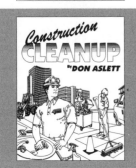

CLEANING!:

NEW REVISION!

CLUTTER:

MORE MAINTENANCE:

MOTIVATION & BUSINESS:

NEW

PROFESSIONAL CLEANERS:

VIDEOS:

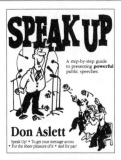

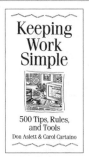

NEW RELEASE!

Mail your order to:
Don Aslett
PO Box 700
Pocatello ID 83204

Phone orders call:
208-232-3535

☐ Don, please put my name and the enclosed list of friends of mine on your mailing list for the *Clean Report* bulletin and catalog.

TITLE	Retail	Qty	Amt
Clean In A Minute	$5.00		
Video Clean In A Minute	$12.95		
●Cleaning Up For a Living	$16.99		
Clutter Free! Finally & Forever	$12.99		
Clutter's Last Stand	$11.99		
●Construction Cleanup	$19.95		
Do I Dust or Vacuum First?	$3.99		
Don Aslett's Stainbuster's Bible	$11.95		
Everything I Needed to Know...Barnyard	$9.95		
How to Be #1 With Your Boss	$9.99		
How to Handle 1,000 Things at Once	$12.99		
How to Have a 48-Hour Day	$12.99		
●How to Upgrade & Motivate Your Crew	$19.95		
Is There Life After Housework?	$10.99		
Video Is There Life After Housework?	$19.95		
Keeping Work Simple	$9.95		
Make Your House Do the Housework	$14.99		
Not For Packrats Only	$11.95		
Painting Without Fainting	$9.99		
Pet Clean-Up Made Easy	$12.99		
●Professional Cleaner's Clip Art	$19.95		
Speak Up	$12.99		
The Cleaning Encyclopedia	$15.95		
The Office Clutter Cure	$9.99		
●The Pro. Cleaner's Handbook	$10.00		
Who Says It's A Woman's Job	$5.95		
Wood Floor Care	$7.95		
You Can You Should Write Poetry	$10.00		
●**Pro Library** ALL 5 ● BOOKS above	$86.84 Only $69.95		

Shipping: $3 for first book or video plus 75¢ for each additional.	Subtotal	
	Idaho res. add 5% Sales Tax	
	Shipping	
	TOTAL	

☐ Enclosed ☐ Visa ☐ MasterCard ☐ Discover ☐ American Express

Card No. _____ Exp Date _____

Signature X _____

Ship to:
Your Name _____ Phone _____

Street Address _____

City ST Zip _____

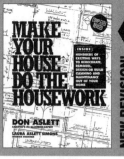

VIDEOS:

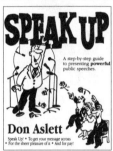

NEW RELEASE!

TITLE	Retail	Qty	Amt
Clean In A Minute	$5.00		
Video Clean In A Minute	$12.95		
●Cleaning Up For a Living	$16.99		
Clutter Free! Finally & Forever	$12.99		
Clutter's Last Stand	$11.99		
●Construction Cleanup	$19.95		
Do I Dust or Vacuum First?	$3.99		
Don Aslett's Stainbuster's Bible	$11.95		
Everything I Needed to Know...Barnyard	$9.95		
How to Be #1 With Your Boss	$9.99		
How to Handle 1,000 Things at Once	$12.99		
How to Have a 48-Hour Day	$12.99		
●How to Upgrade & Motivate Your Crew	$19.95		
Is There Life After Housework?	$10.99		
Video Is There Life After Housework?	$19.95		
Keeping Work Simple	$9.95		
Make Your House Do the Housework	$14.99		
Not For Packrats Only	$11.95		
Painting Without Fainting	$9.99		
Pet Clean-Up Made Easy	$12.99		
●Professional Cleaner's Clip Art	$19.95		
Speak Up	$12.99		
The Cleaning Encyclopedia	$15.95		
The Office Clutter Cure	$9.99		
●The Pro. Cleaner's Handbook	$10.00		
Who Says It's A Woman's Job	$5.95		
Wood Floor Care	$7.95		
You Can You Should Write Poetry	$10.00		
●**Pro Library** ALL 5 ● BOOKS above	$86.84 *Only $69.95*		

Mail your order to:
Don Aslett
PO Box 700
Pocatello ID 83204

Phone orders call:
208-232-3535

❑ Don, please put my name and the enclosed list of friends of mine on your mailing list for the *Clean Report* bulletin and catalog.

Shipping: $3 for first book or video plus 75¢ for each additional.	Subtotal	
	Idaho res. add 5% Sales Tax	
	Shipping	
	TOTAL	

❑ Enclosed ❑ Visa ❑ MasterCard ❑ Discover ❑ American Express

Card No. _____ Exp Date _____

Signature X _____

Ship to:
Your Name _____ Phone _____

Street Address _____

City ST Zip _____

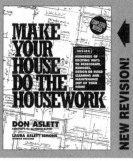

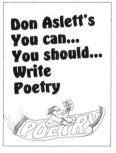